all woman

BLUES

© International Music Publications Ltd
First published in 2002 by International Music Publications Ltd
International Music Publications Ltd is a Faber Music company
Bloomsbury House
74–77 Great Russell Street
London WC1B 3DA
Series Editor: Chris Harvey
Editorial, Production and Recording: Artemis Music Limited
Design and Production: Space DPS Limited
Printed in England by Caligraving Ltd
All rights reserved

ISBN10: 0-571-53225-X
EAN13: 978-0-571-53225-4

FABER *ff* MUSIC

The Birth Of The Blues

Words by Bud De Sylva and Lew Brown
Music by Ray Henderson

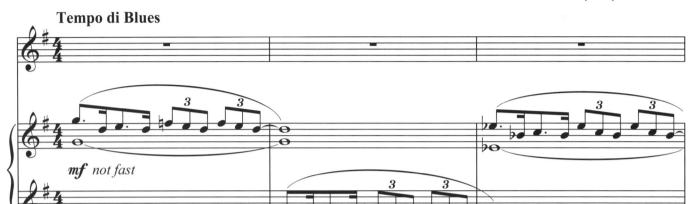

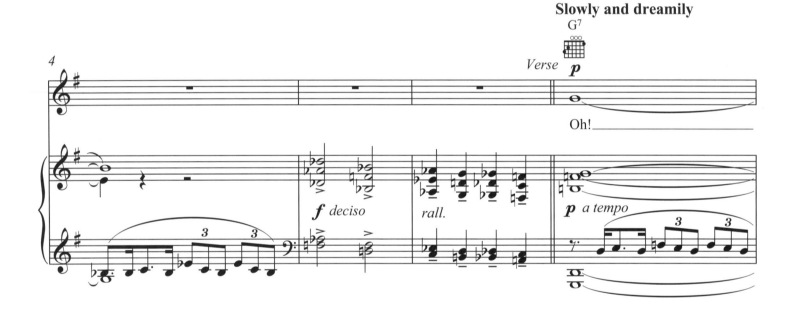

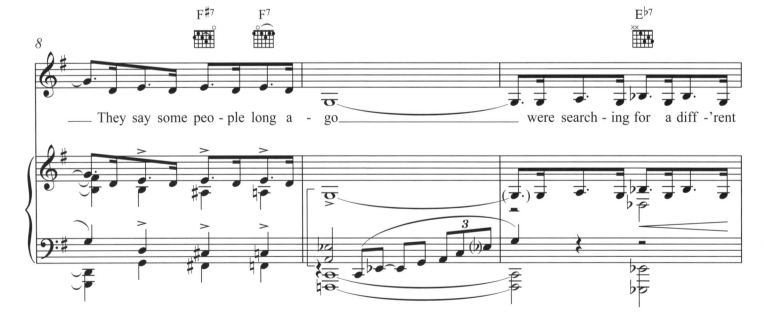

Backing

Come Rain Or Come Shine

Words by Johnny Mercer
Music by Harold Arlen

Freely

Slowly and very tenderly

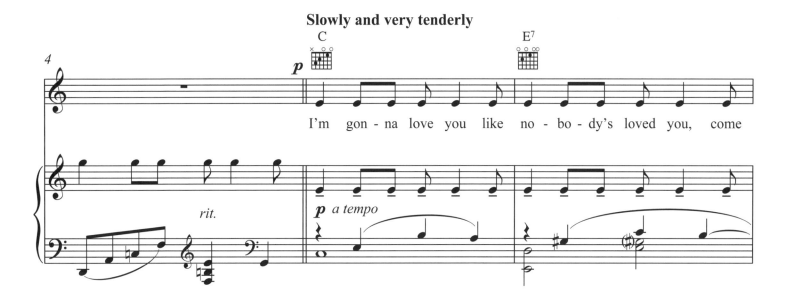

I'm gon - na love you like no - bo - dy's loved you, come

rain or come shine._____ High as a moun - tain and

Backing

Embraceable You

Music and Lyrics by
George Gershwin and Ira Gershwin

Doz - ens of girls would storm____ up;
I went a - bout re - cit - - ing,

I had to lock my door.
Here's one who'll nev - er fall!

Some - how I could - n't warm____ up to
But I'm a - fraid the writ - ing is

one be - fore.
on the wall.

What was it that con - trolled____ me?
My nose I used to turn____ up

Knock On Wood

Words and Music by
Steve Cropper and Eddie Floyd

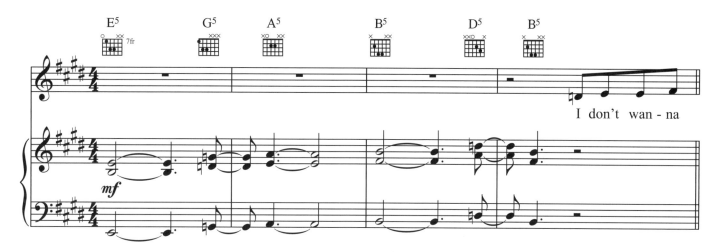

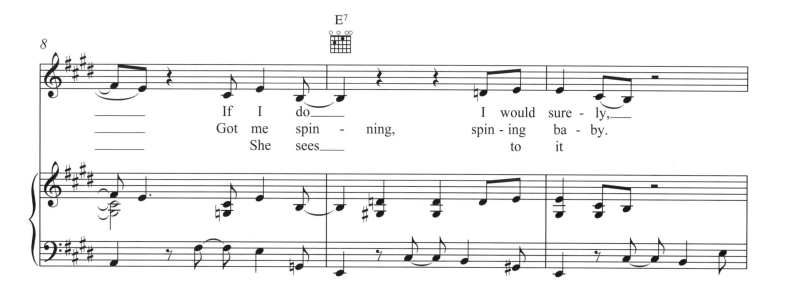

sure - ly lose a lot._____ 'Cause your love_____ is bet -
Ba - by, I'm in a trance._____ 'Cause your love_____ is bet -
that I get e - nough._____ Just one touch_____ from__

- ter than an - y love I___ know._____ It's like thun -
- ter than an - y love I___ know._____
___ her, you know it means so___ much._____

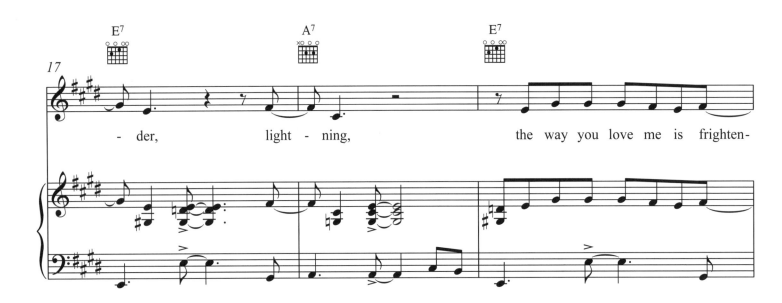

- der, light - ning, the way you love me is frighten-

Georgia On My Mind

Backing

Words by Stuart Gorrell
Music by Hoagy Carmichael

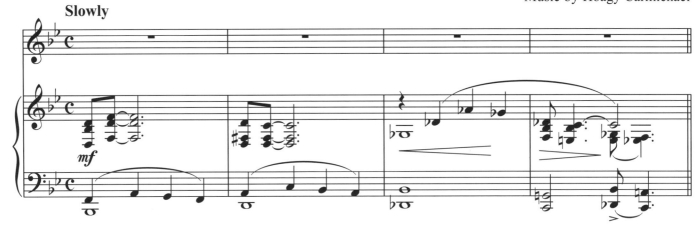

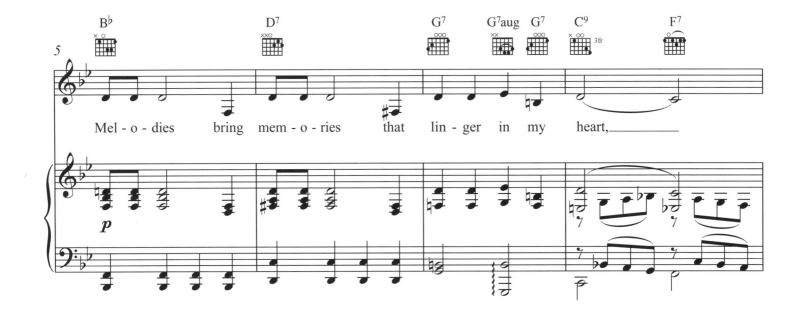

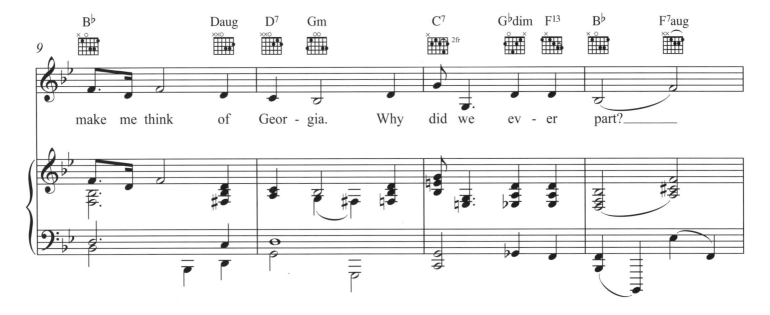

Backing

Mood Indigo

Words and Music by Duke Ellington,
Irving Mills and Albany Bigard

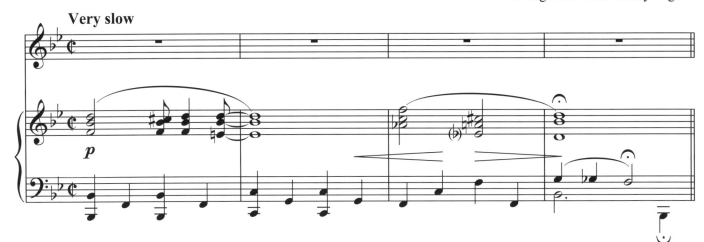

Very slow

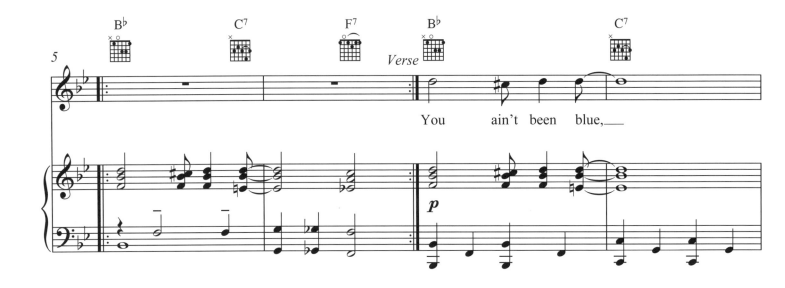

Verse

You ain't been blue,___

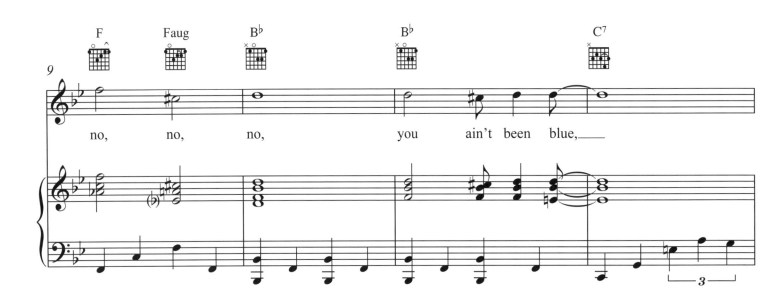

no, no, no, you ain't been blue,___

Night And Day

Words and Music by
Cole Porter

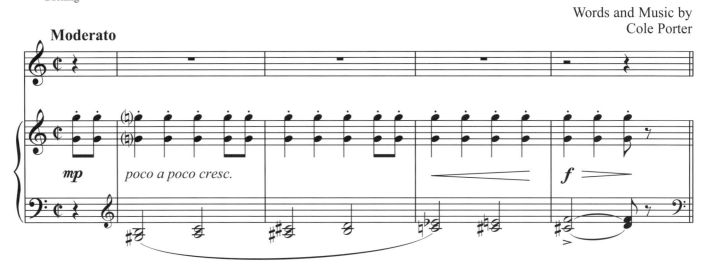

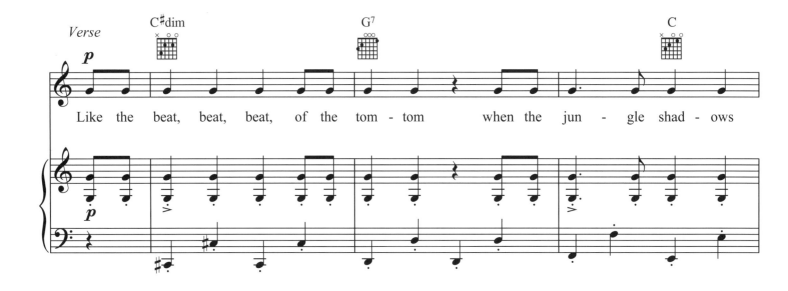

Someone To Watch Over Me

Music and Lyrics by
George Gershwin and Ira Gershwin

There's a say-ing old, say's that love is blind, still we're of-ten told, Seek and

ye shall find. So I'm going to seek a cer-tain lad I've

Rescue Me

Words and Music by
Raymond Smith and Carl Miner

Backing

Stormy Weather

Words by Ted Koehler
Music by Harold Arlen

Slow lament

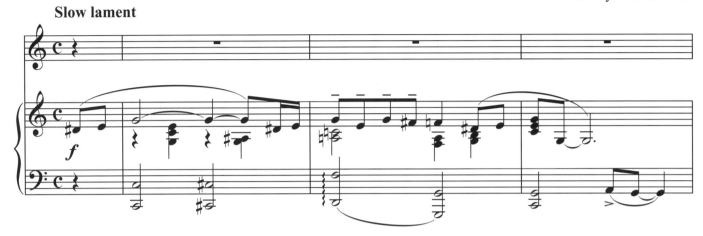

Don't know why_____ there's no sun up in the sky, storm - y

Take Another Little Piece Of My Heart

Words by Bert Berns
Music by Jerry Ragovoy

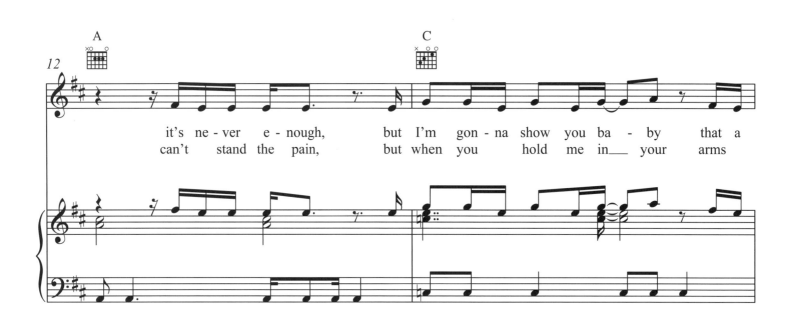

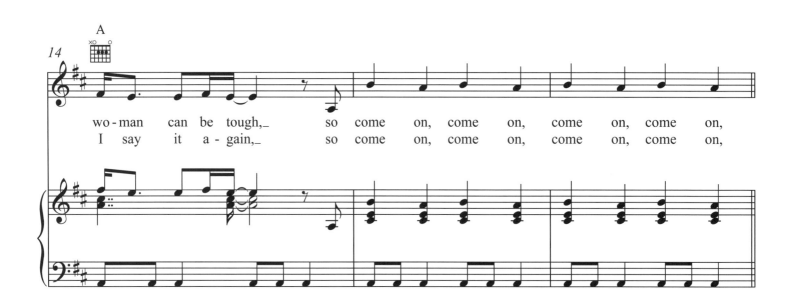

Backing

What Is This Thing Called Love

Words and Music by
Cole Porter

YOU'RE THE VOICE

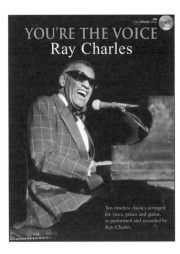

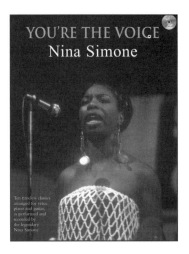

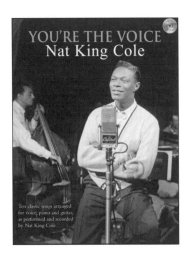

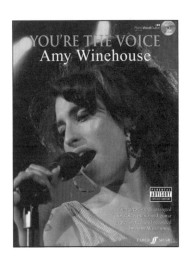

The outstanding vocal series from Faber Music
CD contains full backings for each song,
professionally arranged to recreate the sounds of the original recording

Shirley Bassey · James Blunt · Michael Bublé · Maria Callas · Eva Cassidy · Ray Charles
Nat King Cole · Sammy Davis Jr · Celine Dion · Aretha Franklin · Billie Holiday
Katherine Jenkins · Norah Jones · Tom Jones · Alicia Keys · Carole King · Madonna
George Michael · Dean Martin · Bette Midler · Matt Monro · Nina Simone
Frank Sinatra · Dusty Springfield · Barbra Streisand · Amy Winehouse

To buy Faber Music publications or to find out about the full range of titles available
please contact your local music retailer or Faber Music sales enquiries:

Faber Music Ltd, Burnt Mill, Elizabeth Way, Harlow CM20 2HX
Tel: +44 (0) 1279 82 89 82   Fax: +44 (0) 1279 82 89 83
sales@fabermusic.com   fabermusic.com   expressprintmusic.com

ESSENTIAL AUDITION SONGS

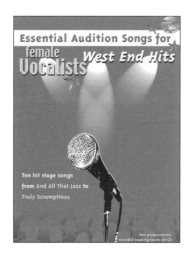

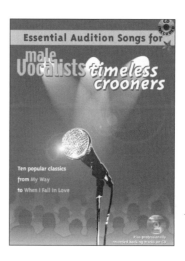

KIDS	**Kids**	MALE	**Broadway**
FEMALE	**Broadway**	MALE	**Pop Ballads**
FEMALE	**Jazz Standards**	MALE	**Timeless Crooners**
FEMALE	**Movie Hits**	MALE & FEMALE	**Comedy Songs**
FEMALE	**Pop Ballads**	MALE & FEMALE	**Duets**
FEMALE	**Pop Divas**	MALE & FEMALE	**Wannabe Pop Stars**
FEMALE	**West End Hits**	MALE & FEMALE	**Love Songs**

FABER *ff* MUSIC

To buy Faber Music publications or to find out about the full range of titles available
please contact your local music retailer or Faber Music sales enquiries:

Faber Music Ltd, Burnt Mill, Elizabeth Way, Harlow CM20 2HX
Tel: +44 (0) 1279 82 89 82   Fax: +44 (0) 1279 82 89 83
sales@fabermusic.com   fabermusic.com   expressprintmusic.com

all woman

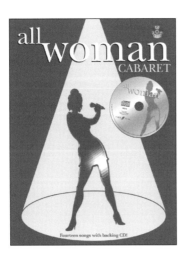

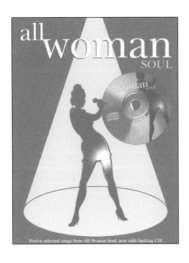
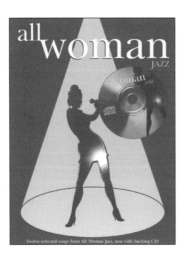
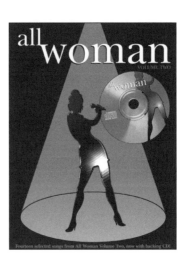

All Woman Collection. Vol.1 WITH CD   All Woman. Love Songs WITH CD
All Woman Collection. Vol.2 WITH CD   All Woman. Jazz WITH CD
All Woman Collection. Vol.3 WITH CD   All Woman. Blues WITH CD
All Woman Collection. Vol.4 WITH CD   All Woman. Soul WITH CD
All Woman. Songbirds WITH CD   All Woman. Cabaret WITH CD
All Woman. Power Ballads WITH CD   All Woman Tearjerkers WITH CD
All Woman Bumper Collection WITH CDs

FABER *ff* MUSIC

To buy Faber Music publications or to find out about the full range of titles available
please contact your local music retailer or Faber Music sales enquiries:

Faber Music Ltd, Burnt Mill, Elizabeth Way, Harlow CM20 2HX
Tel: +44 (0) 1279 82 89 82   Fax: +44 (0) 1279 82 89 83
sales@fabermusic.com   fabermusic.com   expressprintmusic.com